SKILL SHARPENERS
Geography
2

Writing: Rachel D'Orsaneo
Editing: Lisa Vitarisi Mathews
Copy Editing: Cathy Harber
Art Direction: Yuki Meyer
Illustration: Ann Iosa
Design/Production: Jessica Onken

EMC 3742

Evan-Moor.
Helping Children Learn

Visit
teaching-standards.com
to view a correlation
of this book.
This is a free service.

**Correlated to
Current Standards**

CPSIA: Asia Pacific Offset Ltd, Kowloon, Hong Kong [12/2019]

Contents

Places and Regions, *continued*

Physical Systems

Human Systems

Environment and Society

The Uses of Geography

How to Use This Book

Learning About Geography

Children are naturally curious about the world around them. As your child asks questions about the physical world, use the lessons in this book to help your child answer those questions and apply them to his or her everyday life using the basic concepts about maps, globes, places and regions, landforms, bodies of water, and environments that are introduced in the lessons. Connecting your child's real-world experiences to geography concepts and vocabulary will help prepare him or her for success in school.

Reading Selections

Provide support as your child reads the selections. Discuss how the illustrations or photos help your child better understand the geography concept. Help your child make connections between the geography concepts and his or her own life.

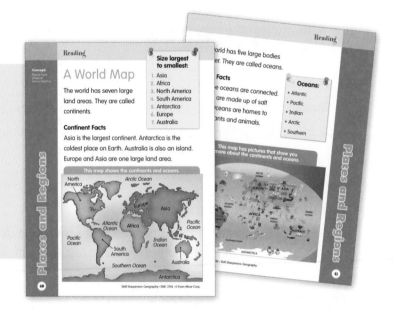

Vocabulary

The vocabulary activities range from word play activities, such as solving clues, to matching vocabulary words to definitions to using vocabulary words to complete sentences. Provide your child with support as he or she completes the activity by answering any questions he or she may have.

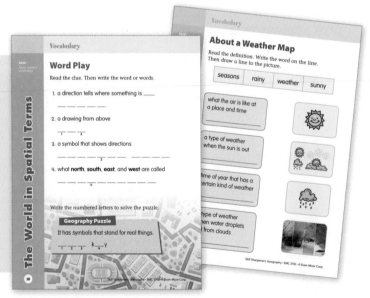

Skill Sharpeners: Geography • EMC 3742 • © Evan-Moor Corp.

Visual Literacy

Illustrations and photos help your child relate geography concepts to the real world. Use the visual literacy activities to reinforce the geography concept that was presented in the reading selection. Provide your child with support as he or she completes the activity.

What I Learned

These activities provide your child with an opportunity to demonstrate an understanding of the geography concepts and vocabulary he or she learn in each unit.

Hands-on Activities

The hands-on activities provide your child with opportunities to connect geography concepts to the real world. The activities focus on developing knowledge of:

- map skills, such as cardinal directions and using a map grid
- the physical world, such as the number of continents and oceans and distinguishing landforms and bodies of water
- human systems, such as population and how people use land
- natural resources, such as gold and oil
- many other important geography concepts

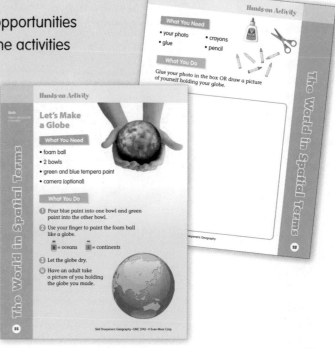

Concept:
A map is a picture from above that shows locations of places and things.

The World in Spatial Terms

What Is a Map?

A map is a drawing of a place from above. A map can show all or parts of Earth. This map shows a place on Earth. It is the country of Canada.

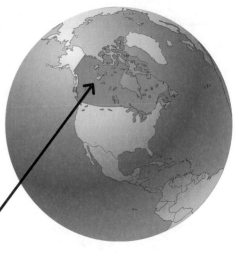

CANADA

Northwest Territories

Yukon

Nunavut

Newfoundland and Labrador

British Columbia

Alberta

Saskatchewan

Manitoba

Ontario

Québec

Prince Edward Island

Ottawa ★

Nova Scotia

New Brunswick

8

A Compass Rose and a Map Key

A compass rose is a symbol that shows directions on a map. A direction shows where something is found. **North**, **south**, **east**, and **west** are directions.

Australia

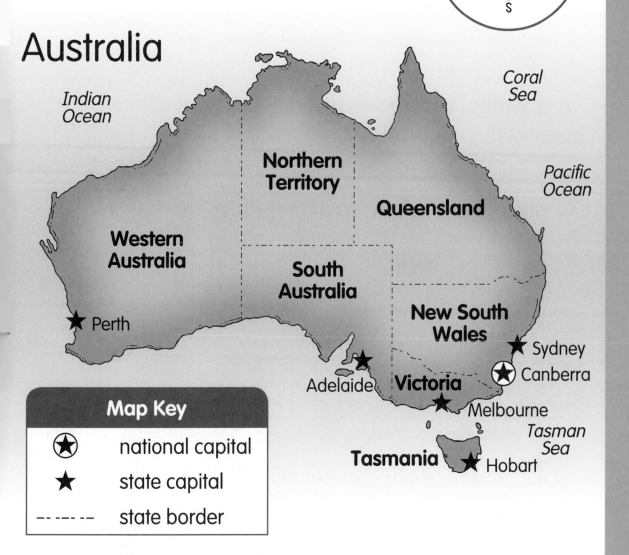

Indian Ocean

Coral Sea

Northern Territory

Queensland

Pacific Ocean

Western Australia

South Australia

New South Wales

★ Perth

Sydney

Canberra

Adelaide

Victoria

Melbourne

Tasman Sea

Tasmania

Hobart

Map Key

⊛	national capital
★	state capital
– – – – – –	state border

A map key has symbols that stand for real things. A map key helps people find things on a map.

The World in Spatial Terms

The World in Spatial Terms

Skill:
Apply content vocabulary

Word Play

Read the clue. Then write the word or words.

1. a direction tells where something is __a__
   __f o u n d__

2. a drawing from above
   __m a p__
   ¹   ³

3. a symbol that shows directions
   __c o m p a s s   r o s s__
              ²

4. what **north**, **south**, **east**, and **west** are called
   __d i r e c t i o n s__
   ¹   ⁴

Write the numbered letters to solve the puzzle.

Geography Puzzle

It has symbols that stand for real things.

__m a p__   k e y
¹ ² ³   ⁴

Skill Sharpeners: Geography • EMC 3742 • © Evan-Moor Corp.

Skill:
Demonstrate an understanding of geography concepts

Map Sentences

Mark the sentence that goes with each picture.

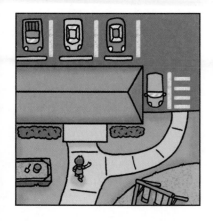

☒ A map is a drawing from above.

☐ A map is a photo from above.

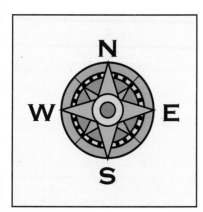

☐ There are five directions on a compass rose.

☒ **North**, **south**, **east**, and **west** are directions.

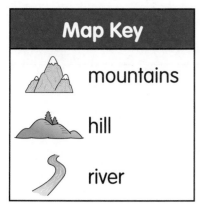

☐ A map key shows directions.

☒ A map key has symbols that stand for real things.

The World in Spatial Terms

Skill:
Apply content
vocabulary

I Know About Maps

Write a sentence about each picture.

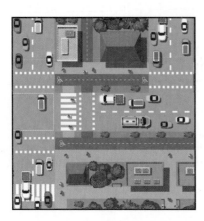

This is a drawing
from above but you
can call it a map.

A map key has little
picatures of real things.

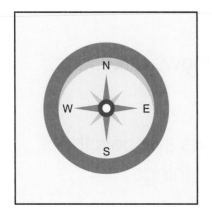

Cempasses tell you
what direction your
going

The World in Spatial Terms

12

A Compass Rose

Skill:
Apply content
knowledge

What You Need

- scissors
- pin or brad
- glue

What You Do

1 Cut out the circle and the arrow.

2 Cut out the letters. Glue them in the correct squares to make a compass rose.

3 Put the arrow on the black dot. Put a pin or brad in it.

4 Use the compass rose to play the game on page 15.

The World

tial Terms

Let's Play

1 You are going on a road trip. You are in Utah. Spin the compass rose.

2 Say the direction the arrow is pointing to.

3 Circle the state you will drive to.

4 Write where you will go.

5 Repeat two or more times.

The World in Spatial Terms

The first place I will go is _Nevada_.

The second place I will go is _Utah_.

The third place I will go is _Wyoming_.

What Is a Globe?

A globe is a model of Earth. It is round like Earth. A globe shows the continents. Continents are large areas of land. Each one is a different shape. There are seven continents. They are:

- Africa
- Antarctica
- Asia
- Australia
- Europe
- North America
- South America

The World in Spatial Terms

North America

Pacific Ocean

Atlantic Ocean

South America

continents

A globe shows the oceans. Oceans are large bodies of salt water. There are five oceans:

- Atlantic Ocean
- Pacific Ocean
- Indian Ocean
- Arctic Ocean
- Southern Ocean

This shows the other side of the globe.

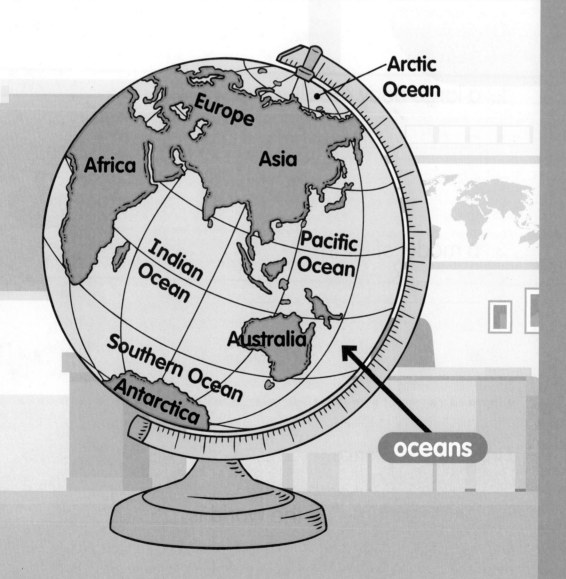

The World in Spatial Terms

Skill:
Apply content
vocabulary

About a Globe

Draw a line to match the picture with the correct definition. Then write the word on the line.

continent	globe	ocean

1. a large area of land

   continent

2. a large body of salt water

   ocean

3. a model of Earth

   globe

Finish the sentence.

4. Another name for the world is *earth*.

The World in Spatial Terms

Skill Sharpeners: Geography • EMC 3742 • © Evan-Moor Corp.

What Is the Picture?

Write a word to go with the picture.

| Earth | continent | ocean | globe |

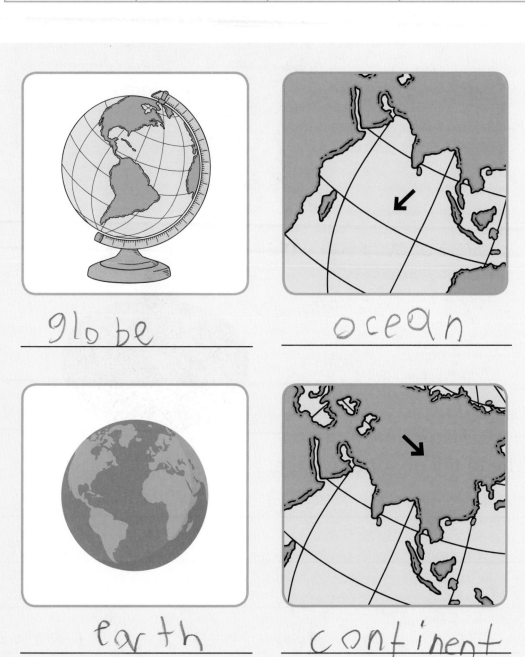

globe

ocean

earth

continent

© Evan-Moor Corp. • EMC 3742 • Skill Sharpeners: Geography

The World in Spatial Terms

Skill:
Write to demonstrate an understanding of geography concepts

All About the Globe

Label the picture of the globe.

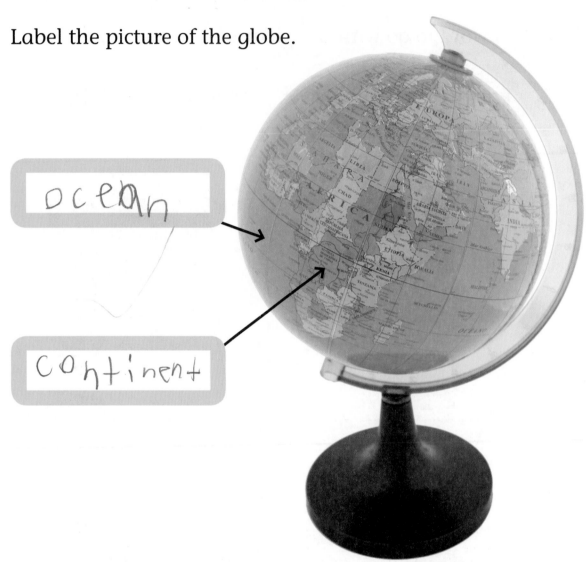

ocean

continent

Write to tell about the globe.

The globe has 5 oceans and 7 continents.

STOP

Skill Sharpeners: Geography • EMC 3742 • © Evan-Moor Corp.

The World in Spatial Terms

Find a Globe

A globe is round like Earth.

What You Do

1 Find things where you live that look like a globe.

2 Draw them in the box.

3 Write the name of each item below the picture.

Skill:
Apply geography concepts

The World in Spatial Terms

Skill:
Apply geography concepts

Let's Make a Globe

What You Need

- foam ball
- 2 bowls
- green and blue tempera paint
- camera (optional)

What You Do

1. Pour blue paint into one bowl and green paint into the other bowl.

2. Use your finger to paint the foam ball like a globe.

   = oceans   = continents

3. Let the globe dry.

4. Have an adult take a picture of you holding the globe you made.

The World in Spatial Terms

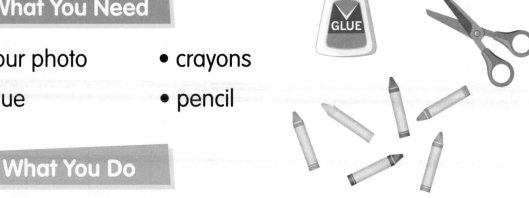

What You Need

- your photo
- glue
- crayons
- pencil

What You Do

Glue your photo in the box OR draw a picture of yourself holding your globe.

The World in Spatial Terms

Concept:

Map grids help people locate places on a map.

The World in Spatial Terms

A Map Grid

A grid is a pattern of lines. The lines form squares.

To talk about a grid square:

- say the letter first

- say the number second

	1	2	3	4
A	🌳			
B				
C			🐕	
D				

Where is the tree?

The tree is at **A1**.

Map grids help people use maps. People can use a map grid to find places on a map or to say where something is.

Skill Sharpeners: Geography • EMC 3742 • © Evan-Moor Corp.

This map shows the state of Ohio in a grid. The dark black line around the state shows its borders. Borders show where a place begins and ends.

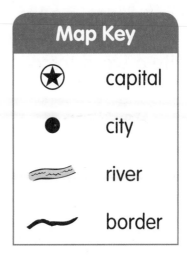

Map Key

⭐ capital

● city

〜 river

〜 border

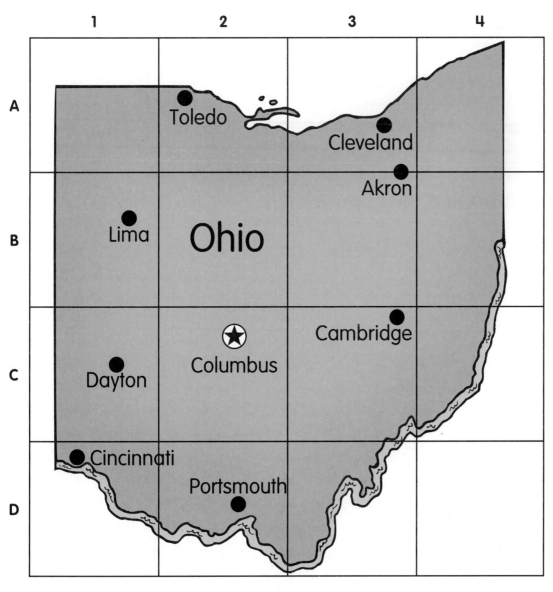

The World in Spatial Terms

The World in Spatial Terms

Use Vocabulary

Write a word to complete each sentence.

capital	border	city	river

1. A ___river___ is a large stream of water that flows across land.

2. Columbus is the ___capital___ of Ohio.

3. A ___border___ shows where a place begins and ends.

4. A ___city___ is a large or important town.

....

Trace the grid.

Draw a ▲ in **A2**.

Draw a ☆ in **D1**.

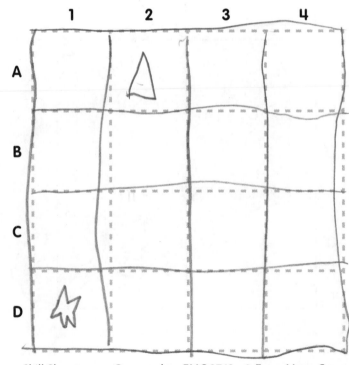

Using a Map Grid

Skill:
Use a map grid

Use the map grid to answer the questions.

1. What animals are in **C4**?

2. What animals are in **B2**?

3. Where is the entrance?

4. Where can you buy ice cream?

5. Trace the square around the tigers.

crocadile
Hippos
D2
B4

The World in Spatial Terms

Map Grid Facts

Follow the directions.

1. Circle the borders in **A2**.

2. Draw a boat in **D3**.

3. Underline the city in **B4**.

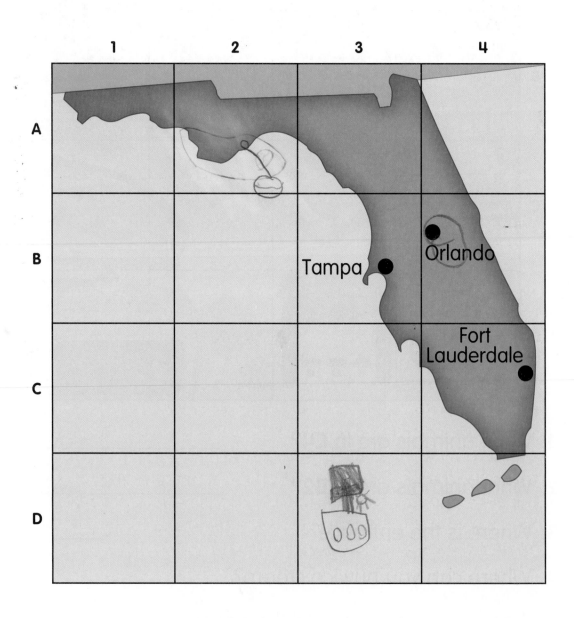

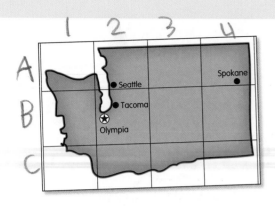

Glue the grid squares together to make the state of Washington.

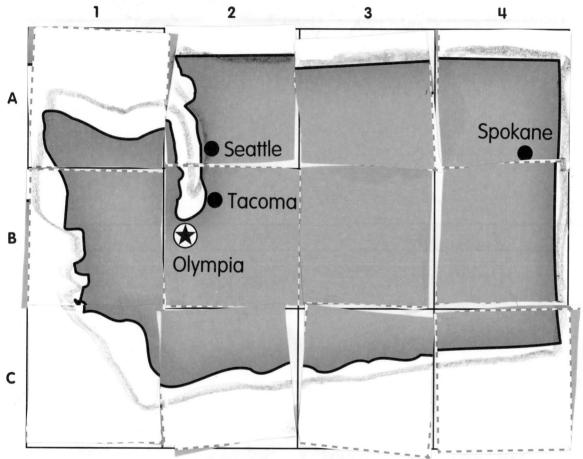

Trace the border in red.
Write the letter and number for each city.

Seattle __A 2__   Spokane __A 4__

Tacoma __B 2__   Olympia __B 2__

STOP

Concept:
Road maps show routes people can use to travel to different locations.

A Road Map

A **road map** shows highways.
A **highway** is a main road.

This is the highway symbol.

Cars, trucks, and buses travel on highways and interstates.

People plan a **route** when they travel.
A route is a way to go from one place to another.

Nebraska

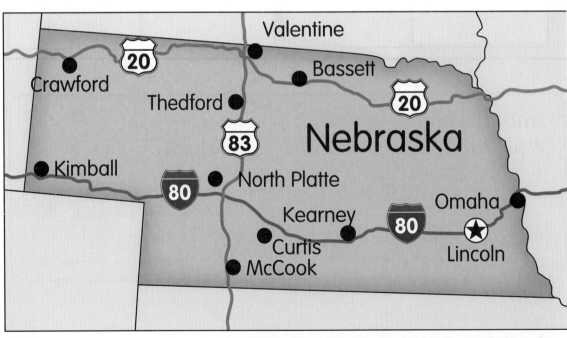

The World in Spatial Terms

South Dakota is a state. It has lots of roads that cross the state. Four highways are shown on this map. Some cities are shown along the highways.

There are a lot of cities in South Dakota. This map shows some of them.

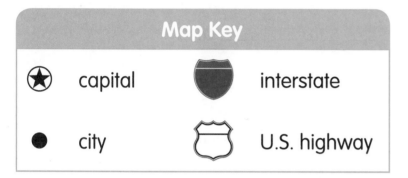

The World in Spatial Terms

33

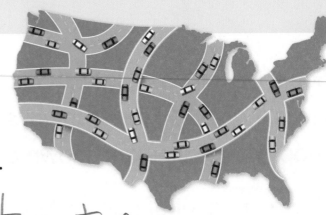

Word Play

Read the clue. Then
write the word or words.

1. Nebraska is a __s t a t e__.
                        3

2. Cars, trucks, and buses travel on
   __h i g h w a y s__ and
                    4
   __i n t e r s t a t e s__.

3. A way to go from one place to another
   is a __r o u t e__.
         1   2

Write the numbered letters to solve the puzzle.

Geography Puzzle

It shows highways people travel on.

__r o a d__ d __m a p__
 1   2   3   4

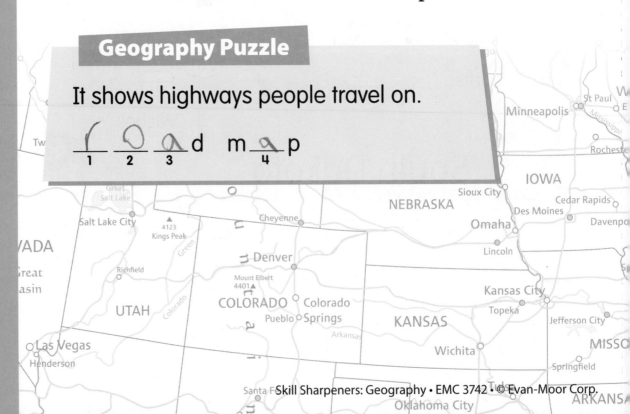

The World in Spatial Terms

What's the Symbol?

Skill:
Demonstrate an
understanding
of geography
concepts

Write the name of each symbol.

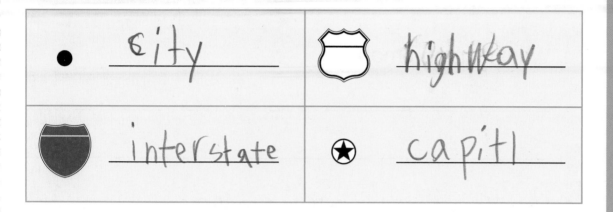

●	_city_	⬡	_highway_
🛡	_interstate_	★	_capitl_

Find each symbol on the map.

Circle ● in green.

Circle ⬡ in red.

Circle 🛡 in blue.

Circle ★ in orange.

The World in Spatial Terms

NO ✓

Road Map Facts

Write to tell what facts you
learned about road maps.

Do Alone - use page

1. What is a road map? 32

_____

_____

2. How does a road map help people?

_____

_____

3. Why are highways important?

_____

_____

Draw a road map.

```
┌─────────────────────────────────┐
│                                 │
│                                 │
│                                 │
│                                 │
│                                 │
│                                 │
└─────────────────────────────────┘
```

The World in Spatial Terms

36

Road Map Clues

Skill:
Apply geography concepts in context

What You Need

- scissors
- crayons
- glue

What You Do

1. Cut out the city names, road symbols, and compass rose.

2. Follow the directions on page 39.

Phoenix | Mesa | Tucson

40 | 60 | 10

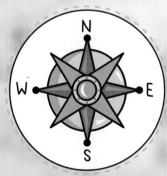

The World in Spatial Terms

Glue the compass rose in the circle. Then read the clues and glue each label in the correct place on the map.

1. Tucson is the city farthest south.

2. Phoenix is the city farthest north.

3. Mesa is the city nearest to Phoenix.

4. Highway 60 runs through Phoenix and Mesa.

5. Interstate 40 runs west to east.

6. Interstate 10 runs through Tucson and Phoenix.

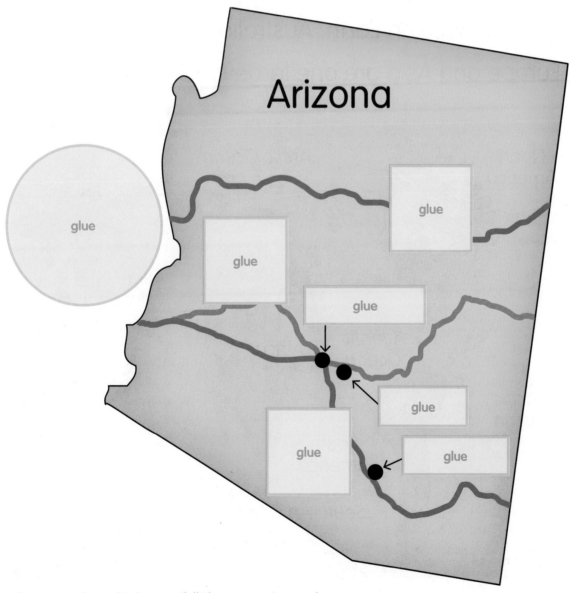

Concept:

Places have physical characteristics.

A World Map

The world has seven large land areas. They are called continents.

Continent Facts

Asia is the largest continent. Antarctica is the coldest place on Earth. Australia is also an island. Europe and Asia are one large land area.

Size largest to smallest:

1. Asia
2. Africa
3. North America
4. South America
5. Antarctica
6. Europe
7. Australia

This map shows the continents and oceans.

North America

Arctic Ocean

Europe

Asia

Atlantic Ocean

Africa

Pacific Ocean

Pacific Ocean

Indian Ocean

South America

Australia

Southern Ocean

Antarctica

Places and Regions

Skill Sharpeners: Geography • EMC 3742 • © Evan-Moor Corp.

The world has five large bodies of water. They are called oceans.

Ocean Facts

All of the oceans are connected. Oceans are made up of salt water. Oceans are homes to many plants and animals.

Oceans:

- Atlantic
- Pacific
- Indian
- Arctic
- Southern

This map has pictures that show you more about the continents and oceans.

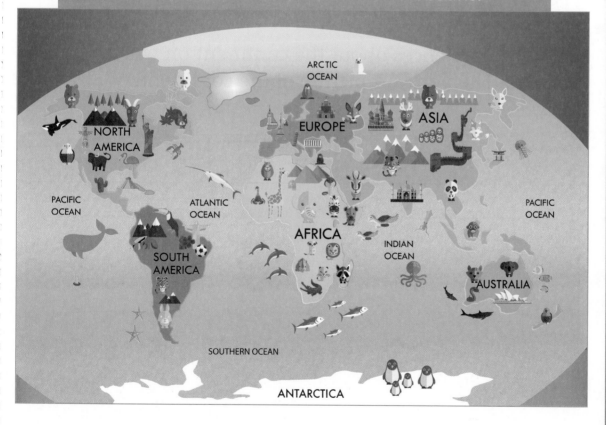

Use Vocabulary

Write a word to complete each sentence.

ocean	world	continent

1. A _____ is one of the seven large areas of land.

2. The _____ is another word for the Earth.

3. An _____ is a large body of salt water.

Write two sentences about the continent on which you live. Then draw a picture of the continent.

_____

_____

Places and Regions

Map Facts

Skill:
Demonstrate an understanding of geography concepts

Mark the sentences that are true.

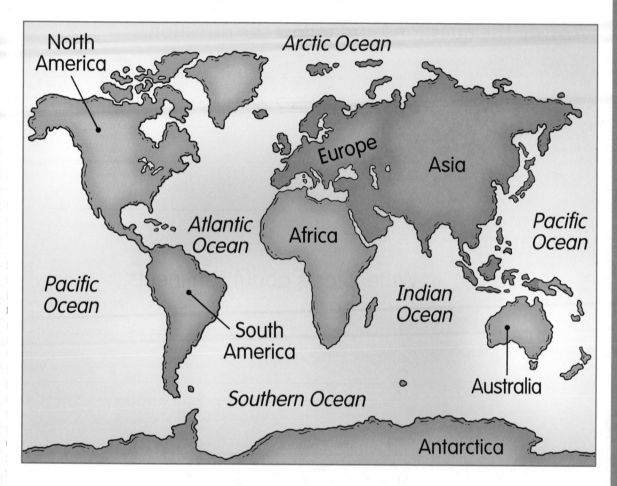

☐ Australia is the only continent that is also an island.

☐ North America and South America are connected.

☐ Europe and Asia are not connected.

☐ Africa is the smallest continent.

☐ Antarctica is not connected to any other continent.

Places and Regions

Skill:
Apply content
vocabulary

Oceans and Continents on a World Map

Answer the questions and follow the directions.

continents

What are the 7 continents?

_____

_____

Write 2 facts about continents.

1. _____

2. _____

oceans

What are the 5 oceans?

_____

_____

Write 2 facts about oceans.

1. _____

2. _____

Places and Regions

Skill Sharpeners: Geography • EMC 3742 • © Evan-Moor Corp.

Make a World Map

Skill:
Apply geography concepts in context

What You Need

What You Do

- scissors

- glue

Cut out the continents. Glue them onto page 47 to finish the map.

Places and Regions

45

Glue each continent in the correct place.

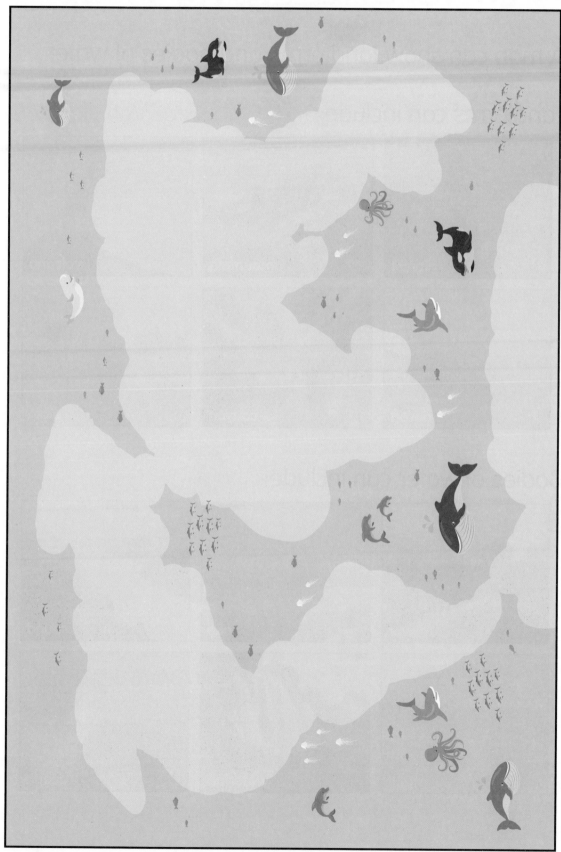

Concept:
Places have physical characteristics.

A Land and Water Map

A map can show landforms and bodies of water.

Landforms can include:

forest

mountain

volcano

desert

canyon

plain

Bodies of water can include:

river

lake

sound

gulf

waterfall

ocean

Skill Sharpeners: Geography • EMC 3742 • © Evan-Moor Corp.

A Land and Water Map of Washington

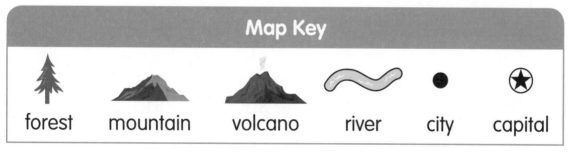

Map Key

| forest | mountain | volcano | river | city | capital |

Washington is a state in the United States. It is called "The Evergreen State." It has landforms such as mountains and volcanoes. Mount Rainier is the highest mountain in Washington. Mount Saint Helens is a famous volcano there. Washington also has bodies of water. Puget Sound is a long body of water. Ships come into Puget Sound.

Places and Regions

About a Land and Water Map

Write a word to match each picture and definition.

landform	river	sound	volcano

1. 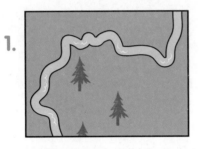 a large stream of water that flows across land

_____

2.  a mountain with an opening at the top

_____

3.  the shape of land, such as a mountain

_____

4.  a long waterway between two larger bodies of water

_____

Places and Regions

Using a Land and Water Map

Skill:
Apply geography concepts

Use the map to answer the questions.

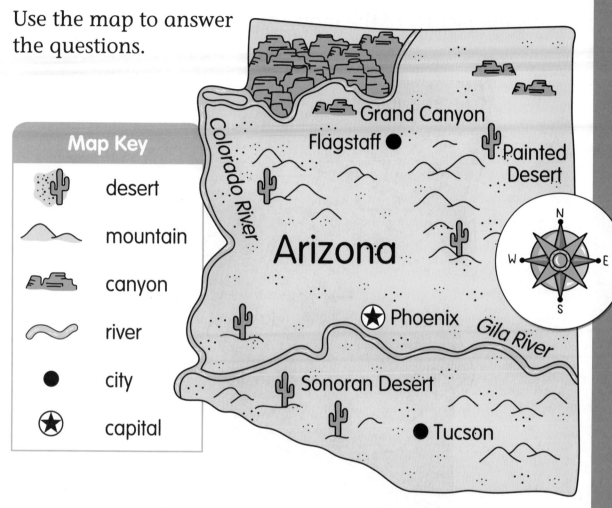

Map Key

desert	
mountain	
canyon	
river	
●	city
★	capital

1. What landform is north of Flagstaff? _____

2. What landform is east of Tucson? _____

3. What river runs north to south? _____

4. In what direction does the
   Gila River run? _____

5. What city is the capital of Arizona? _____

Places and Regions

Skill:
Demonstrate an understanding of geography concepts

All About a Land and Water Map

Label the picture of the map.

Write to tell about the map.

_____

_____

_____

_____

Skill Sharpeners: Geography • EMC 3742 • © Evan-Moor Corp.

Landforms and Bodies of Water

Skill:
Apply geography concepts

What You Need

- scissors
- glue
- pencil

What You Do

Cut out the pictures. Then follow the directions on page 55.

Places and Regions

Places and Regions

Skill Sharpeners: Geography • EMC 3742 • © Evan-Moor Corp.

Sort the pictures into landforms and bodies of water. Then glue the pictures in the boxes and complete the sentences.

You might see these _____ on a map.

glue	glue	glue
glue	glue	glue

You might see these _____ on a map.

glue	glue	glue
glue	glue	glue

Places and Regions

55

A Suburb

A **suburb** is a community near a city.

A **city** is a very large town.

A **community** is a group of people who live together in the same area.

Suburbs have lots of houses. Suburbs also have shopping malls and businesses.

Many people who live in suburbs travel to a city to work.

Look at the map of a suburb. Can you see a big city in the distance?

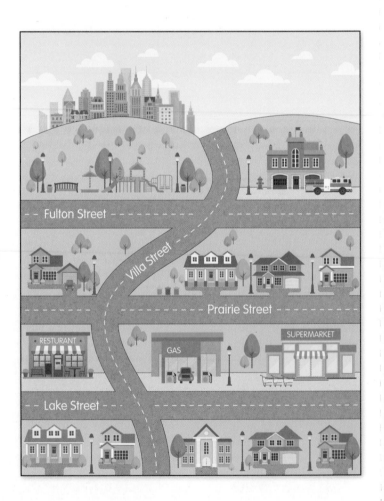

Places and Regions

A City

A **city** is a community where thousands
or millions of people live or work.
A city is a very crowded place.

Cities have a downtown area where
there are many businesses.
There are things like stores, banks,
museums, restaurants, and big companies.
Some companies are in skyscrapers.
A skyscraper is a very tall building.

Neighborhoods, airports,
and factories are not
usually in the
downtown area.

Places and Regions

Word Play

Read the clue. Then write the word.

1. a large or important town

___ ___ ___ ___
 1   5   7

2. a community near a city

___ ___ ___ ___ ___ ___
    3

3. a very tall building

___ ___ ___ ___ ___ ___ ___ ___ ___ ___

4. a city's main business area

___ ___ ___ ___ ___ ___ ___ ___
    2   4   6

Write the numbered letters to solve the puzzle.

Geography Puzzle

It is a group of people who live together in the same area.

___ ___ mm ___ ___ ___ ___ ___
 1   2   3   4   5   6   7

Places and Regions

58

What Is the Picture?

Write a word to go with the picture.

downtown	skyscrapers	city	suburb

_____   _____

_____   _____

Places and Regions

Places People Live and Work

Write a sentence about each picture.

_____

_____

_____

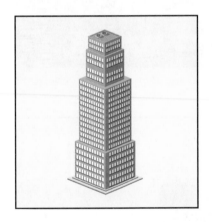

_____

_____

_____

_____

_____

_____

Places and Regions

Skill Sharpeners: Geography • EMC 3742 • © Evan-Moor Corp.

Suburb and City Puzzles

Skill:
Apply geography concepts

What You Need

What You Do

- scissors
- glue

Cut out the puzzle pieces. Put them together to make two puzzles. Glue the puzzles onto page 63.

Places and Regions

This is a suburb.

glue	glue	glue	glue
glue	glue	glue	glue

This is a city.

glue	glue	glue	glue
glue	glue	glue	glue

Places and Regions

Concept:
Regions have physical and human characteristics.

A State Map

A state is a part of a country.

A border can be a line on a map between states or countries. A border shows where places begin and end. Borders can touch land or water.

Ohio

★ Columbus

Every state has a special city. This city is the state capital. A capital is a city where the government of a state or country is found. Columbus is the capital of the state of Ohio.

Places and Regions

64

Map of Georgia

Georgia is a state
in the United States.

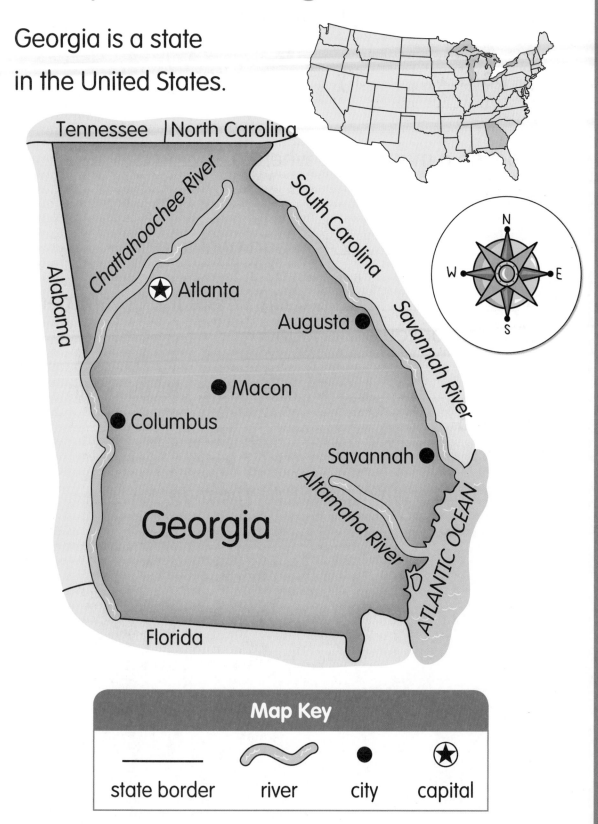

Map Key			
————	∿	●	⊛
state border	river	city	capital

Places and Regions

Use Vocabulary

Write a word to complete each sentence.

border	city	capital	state

1. A dot on a map shows where a _____ is found.

2. A _____ is a part of a country.

3. A _____ is a city where the government of a state or country is found.

4. A _____ shows where places begin and end.

Trace the border of each state on the map.

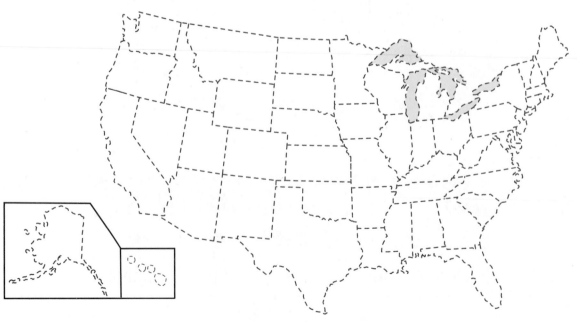

Skill Sharpeners: Geography • EMC 3742 • © Evan-Moor Corp.

Map Sentences

Skill:
Demonstrate an understanding of geography concepts

Mark the sentence that goes with each picture.

☐ The shaded part of this map is a continent.

☐ The shaded part of this map is a state.

☐ The state of Florida has a border that touches land and water.

☐ The state of Florida is the only state that has a border that touches water.

☐ Columbus is a town in Ohio.

☐ Columbus is the capital of Ohio.

Places and Regions

Skill:
Demonstrate an understanding of geography concepts

State Map Facts

Write to tell what you learned about a state map.

1. What is a border?

_____

_____

2. Why does each state have a capital?

_____

_____

3. Why do you think each state has different kinds of communities?

_____

_____

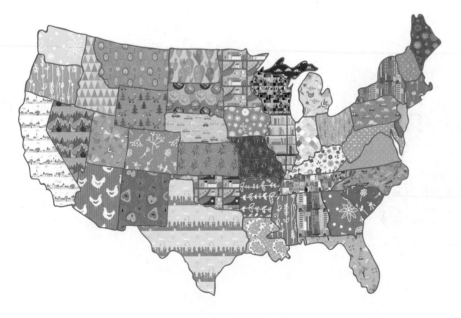

States and Their Capitals

Skill:
Apply geography concepts in context

What You Need

- scissors
- glue

What You Do

1 Cut out the states and stars.

2 Glue them onto page 71.

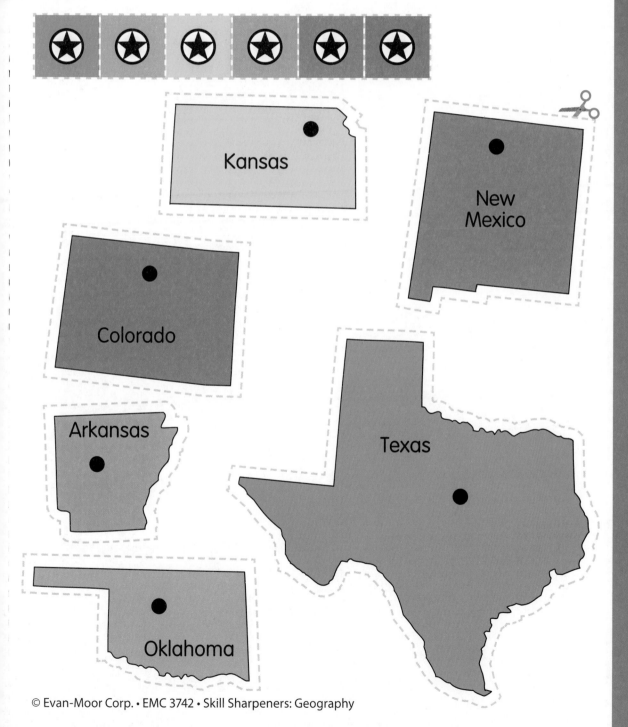

Kansas

New Mexico

Colorado

Arkansas

Texas

Oklahoma

Places and Regions

Places and Regions

Skill Sharpeners: Geography • EMC 3742 • © Evan-Moor Corp.

In the area below, fit the six states together.
Use the outline to match parts of the states' borders.

Glue a star on the dot in each state to show the capital.

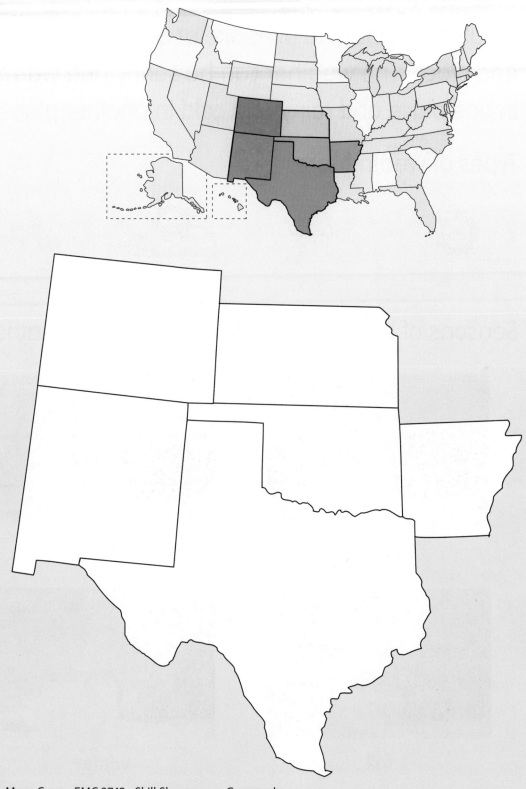

Concept:
Places on Earth have different weather at different times of the year.

A Weather Map

A weather map shows the weather of a place.

Weather is what the air is like at a certain time and place. The weather can be sunny and warm in one place and rainy and cold in another place.

Types of weather are:

Seasons of the year have certain kinds of weather.

summer

spring

fall

winter

Physical Systems

72

Weather Symbols

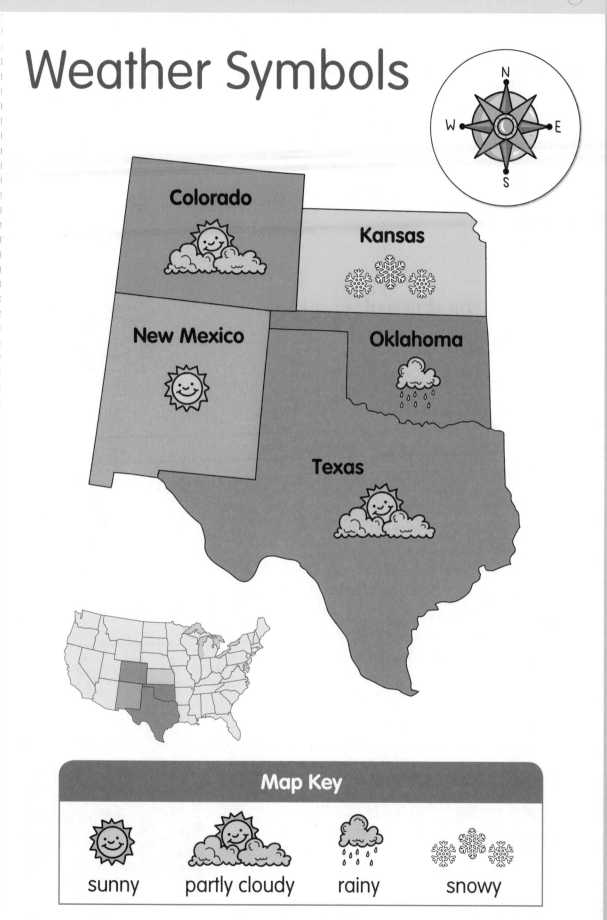

Map Key

sunny   partly cloudy   rainy   snowy

Physical Systems

About a Weather Map

Read the definition. Write the word on the line.
Then draw a line to the picture.

seasons	rainy	weather	sunny

what the air is like at
a place and time

_____

a type of weather
when the sun is out

_____

time of year that has a
certain kind of weather

_____

a type of weather
when water droplets
fall from clouds

_____

Skill Sharpeners: Geography • EMC 3742 • © Evan-Moor Corp.

Skill:
Demonstrate an understanding of geography concepts

Four Seasons

Skill:
Apply geography
concepts

Look at the picture. Write the name of the season.
Then draw a weather symbol.

_____

_____

_____

_____

Physical Systems

Skill:
Apply content vocabulary

Weather and Seasons

Answer the questions and follow the directions.

weather

What are the different kinds of weather?

_____ _____

_____ _____

Write something you know about weather.

_____

_____

seasons

What are the 4 seasons?

_____ _____

_____ _____

Write something you know about seasons.

_____

_____

Physical Systems

Skill Sharpeners: Geography • EMC 3742 • © Evan-Moor Corp.

The Weather Here

Skill:
Apply geography concepts in context

What You Need

- crayons
- scissors
- glue

What You Do

1 Draw a picture of the weather outside your home in the box. Write the kind of weather and the season.

2 Color and cut out the weather symbols.

3 Use the weather symbols on page 79.

weather _____   season _____

Physical Systems

Physical Systems

Use the clues to glue the weather symbols on the correct state.

1. The state west of West Virginia is sunny.

2. The state east of Ohio is snowy.

3. The state north of Kentucky is rainy.

4. The state east of West Virginia is partly cloudy.

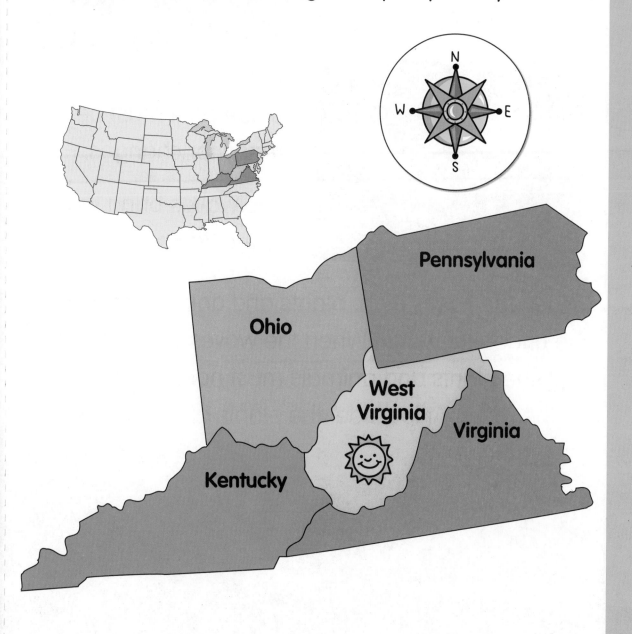

Physical Systems

Concept:
Ecosystems have different characteristics.

An Ocean Habitat

Tide Pools

A tide pool is where the shore and ocean meet. Tide pools can be found all over the world.

Animals and plants in a tide pool must be ready for changes.

The waves bring water to the tide pools.

When the tide is high, plants and animals may be under the water. When the waves go back out, the plants and animals must hold on tight to the rocks. At low tide, the plants and animals may be dry.

Physical Systems

Skill Sharpeners: Geography • EMC 3742 • © Evan-Moor Corp.

Sea otters live in kelp forests.

A Kelp Forest

A kelp forest is a different kind of forest.
Its "trees" are under the water in the ocean.

Kelp is a plant. Many animals live in a kelp forest.

The kelp gets nutrients, or food, through its blade.
A kelp blade is like a leaf on a land plant.

blade

Physical Systems

Word Play

Read the clue. Then write the word or words.

1. they bring water to tide pools

   ___ ___ ___ ___ ___
            4

2. when plants and animals are dry

   ___ ___ ___   ___ ___ ___ ___
        6   1   2

3. kelp gets nutrients through this

   ___ ___ ___ ___ ___
        8   3

4. its trees are under the water

   ___ ___ ___ ___   ___ ___ ___ ___ ___
            5   7   9

Write the numbered letters to solve the puzzle.

Geography Puzzle

It is where the shore and the ocean meet.

___ ___ ___ ___   ___ ___ ___ ___ ___
 1   2   3   4   5   6   7   8   9

82

Skill:
Demonstrate an understanding of geography concepts

Habitat Sentences

Mark the sentence that goes with each picture.

☐ Tide pools are found where the shore and the ocean meet.

☐ Tide pools are found in the middle of the ocean.

☐ Many animals live in kelp forests.

☐ Only sea stars live in kelp forests.

☐ Sea otters live in tide pools.

☐ Sea otters live in kelp forests.

Physical Systems

Skill:
Demonstrate an understanding of geography concepts

It Looks Like This...

Read the sentence. Then draw a picture to match it.

A tide pool is where the shore and the ocean meet.

Kelp is a plant in the ocean.

The ocean is a habitat to many plants and animals.

Physical Systems

Skill Sharpeners: Geography • EMC 3742 • © Evan-Moor Corp.

Ocean Habitat Collage

Skill:
Apply geography concepts

What You Need

- scissors
- glue
- crayons

What You Do

Cut out the pictures. Use them to make a collage on page 87. Draw pictures of your own for the collage, too.

Physical Systems

Skill Sharpeners: Geography • EMC 3742 • © Evan-Moor Corp.

This is an ocean habitat.

Concept:
Population changes over time.

Human Systems

A Population Map

A city is a very large town. A dot on a map shows where a city is found. A capital is a city where the government of a state or country is found. The government is a group of people who help make laws.

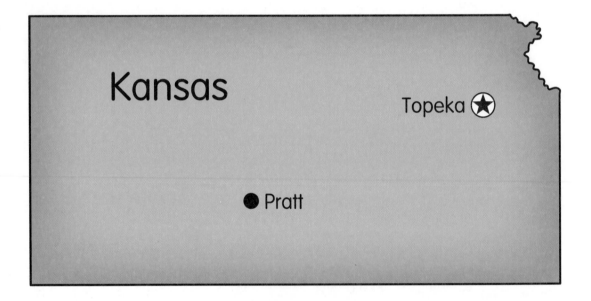

The population is the total number of people who live in a place. Topeka is the capital of the state of Kansas. The population of Topeka is about 127,000. Pratt is a town in Kansas. The population of Pratt is about 7,000. As people move, the population changes.

A Population Map of California

California has the largest population in the United States. Over 39 million people live in California.

Five Largest Cities

1. Los Angeles
2. San Diego
3. San Jose
4. San Francisco
5. Fresno

California

Sacramento ★

San Francisco ●
● San Jose
● Fresno

Pacific
Ocean

● Los Angeles

● San Diego

Human Systems

Skill:
Apply content
vocabulary

Word Play

Read the clue. Then write the word.

1. the total number of people who live in a place

   —— —— —— —— —— —— —— —— —— ——
   1   3

2. a large town   —— —— —— ——

3. a group of people who help make laws

   —— —— —— —— —— —— —— —— —— ——
      9   2   7   6

4. a city where the government of a state or

   country is found   —— —— —— —— —— —— ——
          4   5

5. the capital of Kansas

   —— —— —— —— —— ——
     8   10

Write the numbered letters to solve the puzzle.

Geography Puzzle

It is a reason population changes over time.

—— —— —— —— —— ——   —— —— —— ——
1 2 3 4 5 6   7 8 9 10

Human Systems

Using a Population Map

Skill:
Apply geography concepts in context

Use the map to answer the items.

Australia

Coral Sea

Darwin

Cairns

Townsville

Alice Springs

Brisbane

Canberra

Perth

Sydney

Melbourne

City	Population
Sydney	5 million
Melbourne	4.82 million
Brisbane	2.5 million
Canberra	396,566

1. Which city has the largest population?

   _____

2. Which city has the smallest population?

   _____

3. Which city has a population of 2.5 million?

   _____

4. Circle the name of the capital of Australia.

Human Systems

Skill:
Apply geography concepts in context

All About a Population Map

Look at the map symbols.
Write **capital** and **city** to label the map of Pennsylvania.
Then read the population information.

Pennsylvania

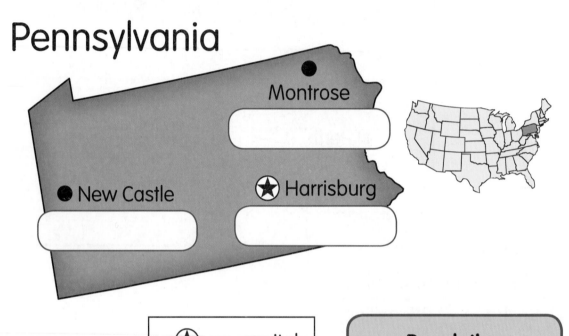

Montrose

New Castle   ⊛ Harrisburg

⊛	capital
●	city
—	border

Population	
Montrose	1,617
New Castle	23,273
Harrisburg	49,528

Write to tell about the state of Pennsylvania.

_____

_____

_____

_____

Skill Sharpeners: Geography • EMC 3742 • © Evan-Moor Corp.

It Means the Same Thing!

Skill:
Demonstrate an understanding of geography concepts

What You Need

- scissors
- glue

What You Do

1 Cut out the cards.

2 Read one card. Find the card on page 95 that means the same thing. Glue the card in the box beside it. You will not use all of the cards.

This city has a large population.	This town has a small population.
This is a very large town.	People moved away from this city over time.
This is the total number of people who live in a place.	This is where the government of a state is found.

Human Systems

population	glue
Fewer than 50 people live in this town.	glue
capital	glue
A lot of people live in this city.	glue

Human Systems

A Product Map of Kansas

Farmers grow crops and raise animals. That is their job. They sell their products to feed people and to earn a living, or make money.

Crops are plants farmers grow for food. Wheat, corn, and sorghum are all grains that can be ground into flour for breads.

Livestock are animals raised on a farm or a ranch. Cattle are cows, bulls, and steers that are raised on a farm or ranch.

Human Systems

A product map shows where things such as crops and livestock are grown or raised to be sold.

Kansas is called "The Wheat State." It grows more wheat than any other state. Kansas is also called "The breadbasket of America."

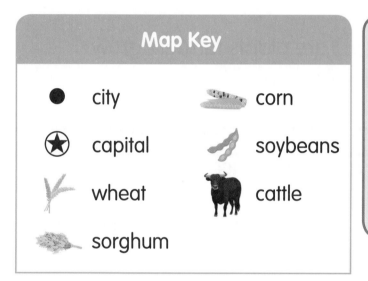

Map Key

●	city		corn
★	capital		soybeans
	wheat		cattle
	sorghum		

Top Farm Products

1. beef cattle
2. wheat
3. corn
4. sorghum grain
5. soybeans

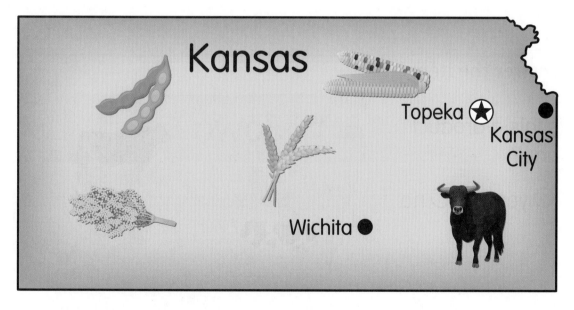

Kansas

Topeka ★

Kansas City

Wichita ●

Human Systems

Skill:
Apply content vocabulary in context sentences

Products

Write a word or words to complete each sentence.

crops	livestock	cattle	product map

1. A _____ shows where things such as crops and livestock are found.

2. _____ are plants farmers grow for food and to sell for money.

3. _____ are cows, bulls, and steers that are raised on a farm or ranch.

4. _____ are animals raised on a farm or ranch. Livestock are sold for money.

....

Answer the item.

Is this a product map?

○ yes   ○ no

Iowa

Skill Sharpeners: Geography • EMC 3742 • © Evan-Moor Corp.

What Is the Picture?

Write a word or words to go with the picture.

crop	livestock	cattle	product map

Skill:
Demonstrate an understanding of geography concepts

_____

_____

_____

_____

Human Systems

Skill:
Demonstrate an understanding of geography concepts

Product Map Facts

Write to tell what you learned about a product map. Explain why farmers grow crops and raise livestock.

1. What is a product map?

   _____

   _____

2. Why do farmers grow crops?

   _____

   _____

3. Where is livestock raised?

   _____

   _____

Human Systems

Skill Sharpeners: Geography • EMC 3742 • © Evan-Moor Corp.

3-D Product Map

Skill:
Apply geography concepts in context

What You Need

- scissors
- glue

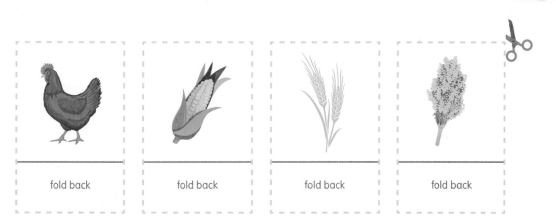

What You Do

1. Cut out the crops and livestock along the dotted lines.

2. Fold back each piece.

3. Follow the directions on page 103.

fold back

fold back

fold back

fold back

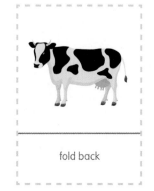

fold back

fold back

fold back

Human Systems

Human Systems

Skill Sharpeners: Geography • EMC 3742 • © Evan-Moor Corp.

Glue the crops and livestock to make a product map. Then complete the sentence.

This is a product map of _____.

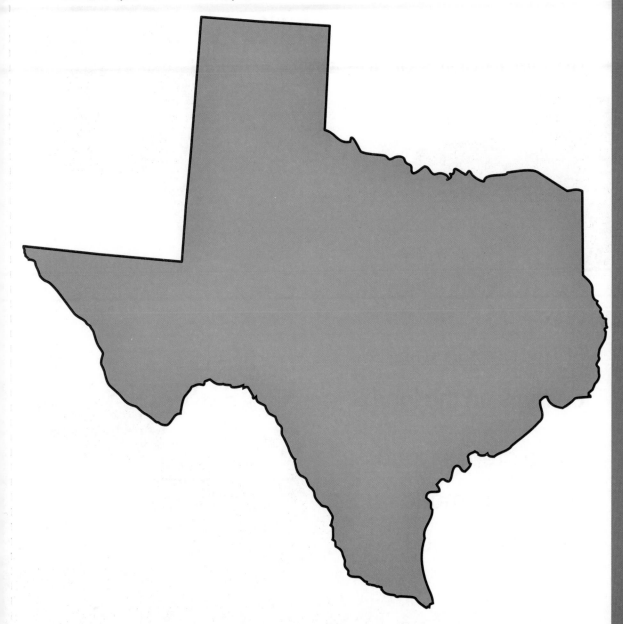

Write about the product map you made.

_____

_____

Human Systems

Concept:
People use land
in different ways.

How People Use Land

Different communities use land in different
ways. Some people grow fruits
and vegetables on the land.

Some people raise
animals on the land.

Some areas of land
have been made
into national parks.

YELLOWSTONE
NATIONAL
PARK

NATIONAL
PARK
SERVICE

Human Systems

Skill Sharpeners: Geography • EMC 3742 • © Evan-Moor Corp.

People use land to build homes and businesses. They also build schools and parks. The way land is used is an important decision. A decision is a choice you make.

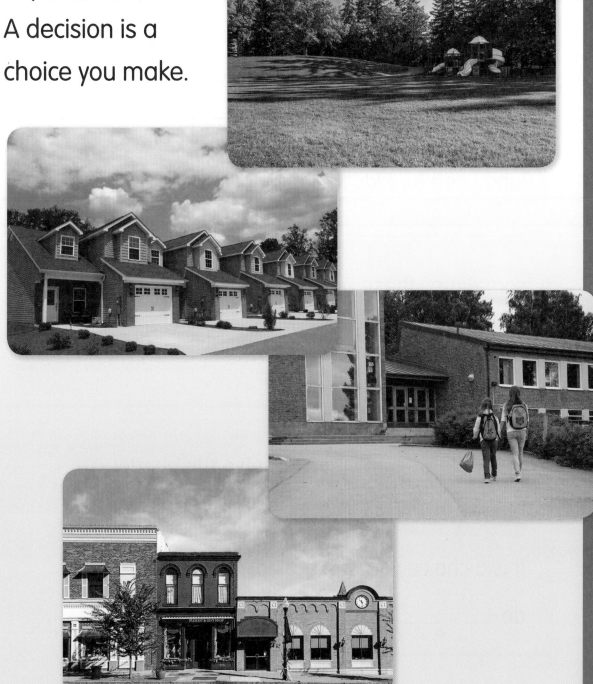

Human Systems

Word Play

Read the clue.
Then write the word.

1. a place where people learn

   __ __ __ __ __ __
     1   5

2. a place where people live and work

   c __ mm __ __ __ ty
                  2

3. land used for kids to play

   __ __ __ __

4. sometimes these are raised
   on a farm

   __ __ __ __ __ __
     6 4   3

Write the numbered letters to solve the puzzle.

Geography Puzzle

It is a choice you make.

de__ __ __ __ __ __
   1 2 3 4 5 6

Land Sentences

Skill:
Demonstrate an understanding of geography concepts

Mark the sentence that goes with each picture.

☐ This land was used to grow fruits.

☐ This land was used to build a community park.

☐ This land was used to raise cattle.

☐ This land was used for a national park.

☐ This land was used to build a community park.

☐ This land was used to raise livestock.

Human Systems

Skill:
Apply geography concepts to real-world situations

All About How Land Is Used

Draw a picture of one way your community uses land.

Write to tell about your picture.

_____

_____

_____

_____

Human Systems

Skill Sharpeners: Geography • EMC 3742 • © Evan-Moor Corp.

How Would You Use the Land?

Skill:
Apply geography concepts to real-world situations

What You Need

- scissors
- glue
- crayons

What You Do

1 Cut out the pictures.

2 Use them on page 111.

Human Systems

Pretend there is a lot of unused land in your area. Glue the pictures and draw to show how you would use the land.

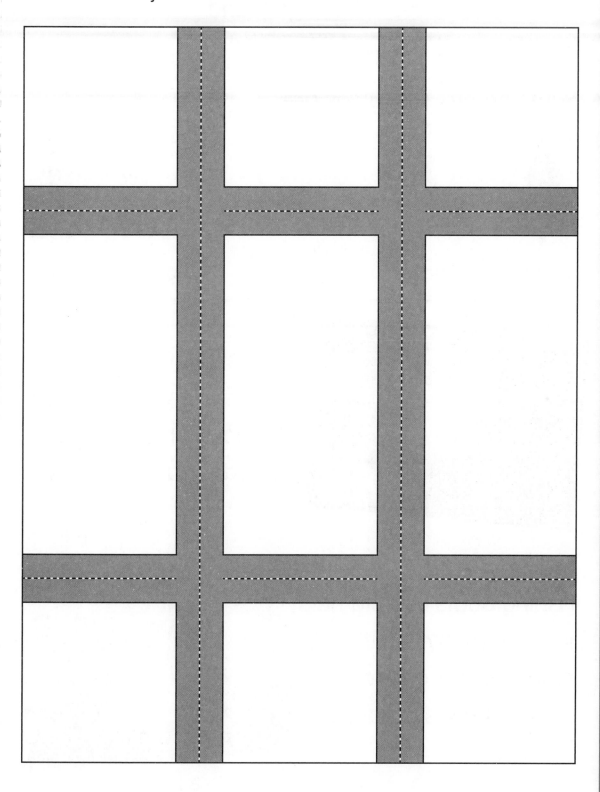

Human Systems

Concept:
Natural resources are found in many places on Earth.

Environment and Society

A Resource Map

Natural resources are things found in nature that are useful to people.

Some natural resources are:

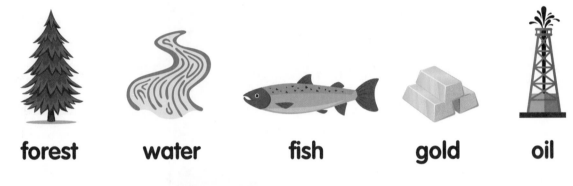

| **forest** | **water** | **fish** | **gold** | **oil** |

Forests have many trees. The wood is used to make products such as paper and furniture.

Fishing boats use big nets to catch many fish at one time. The fish are sold to stores and restaurants.

Skill Sharpeners: Geography • EMC 3742 • © Evan-Moor Corp.

A Resource Map of Maine

Maine has many natural resources. It has lots of forests, waterways, lobsters, and fish. Maine is called "The Pine Tree State." Maine's state animal is the moose.

Map Key	
🌲	forest
〰	river
⛰	mountain
🦞	lobster
🐟	fish

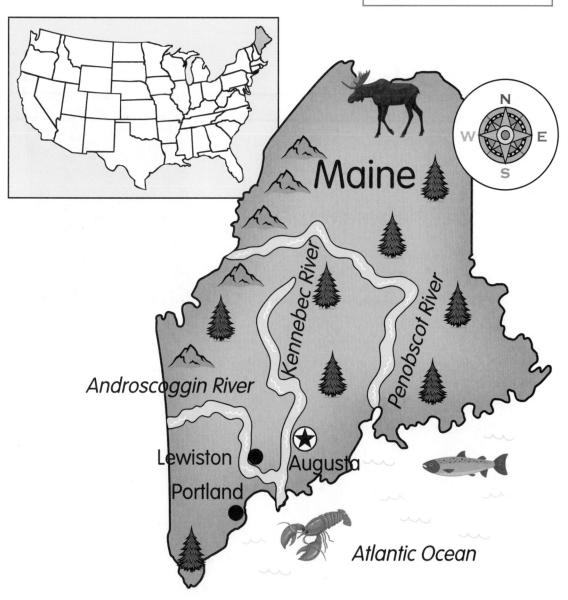

Environment and Society

Skill:
Apply content
vocabulary

Word Play

Read the clue. Then write the word.

1. an area thick with trees

___ ___ ___ ___ ___ ___
$\quad$ 9 $\quad$ 6 $\qquad$ 11 $\quad$ 3

2. a body of water that boats travel on

___ ___ ___ ___ ___ ___ ___ ___
$\quad$ 2 $\qquad$ 10 $\quad$ 4

3. "The Pine Street State"

___ ___ ___ ___
$\quad$ 5 $\quad$ 1 $\quad$ 7

4. a type of natural resource that is found in the ocean

___ ___ ___ ___
$\qquad$ 8

Write the numbered letters to solve the puzzle.

Geography Puzzle

These are things in nature that are useful to people.

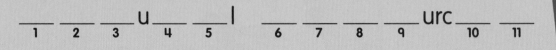

___ ___ ___ u ___ ___ l ___ ___ ___ ___ urc ___ ___
1 $\:$ 2 $\:$ 3 $\quad$ 4 $\:$ 5 $\qquad$ 6 $\:$ 7 $\:$ 8 $\:$ 9 $\qquad$ 10 $\:$ 11

Skill Sharpeners: Geography • EMC 3742 • © Evan-Moor Corp.

What's the Symbol?

Write the name of each symbol.

Find each symbol on the map.
Then complete the sentences.

1. The 🌲 symbol tells
   me that there are

   _____ in the

   _____ half of Peru.

2. The ⛴ symbol tells me that

   there is _____

   near the _____
   border of Peru.

© Evan-Moor Corp. • EMC 3742 • Skill Sharpeners: Geography

Environment and Society

Skill:
Demonstrate an understanding of geography concepts

Environment and Society

Getting Natural Resources

Write a sentence about each picture.

_____

_____

_____

_____

_____

_____

Read. Then answer the question.

This is an oil drilling rig. It is drilling for oil. Oil rigs can be seen all over the world. Have you ever seen an oil drilling rig? Tell where.

_____

_____

Skill Sharpeners: Geography • EMC 3742 • © Evan-Moor Corp.

Natural Resources Puzzle

Skill:
Apply geography concepts

What You Need

- scissors
- glue

What You Do

Cut out the puzzle pieces. Put them together to make a resources world map. Then glue them onto page 119.

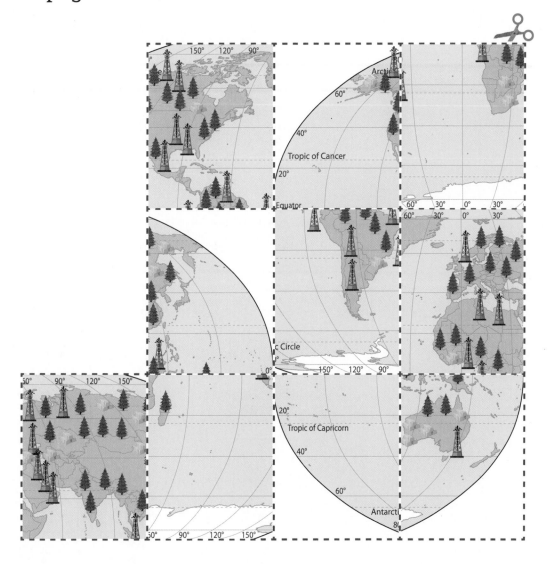

Environment and Society

Resources World Map

glue	glue	glue	glue	glue
glue	glue	glue	glue	glue

Concept:
Places change
over time.

The Uses of Geography

Then and Now

Places change over time. People build new buildings. They make new roads. The place where you live looked different in the past. It will also look different in the future.

The past is the time that happened long ago.

The present is the time that is happening now.

The future is the time that has not happened yet. The future is:

- tomorrow
- next week
- next month
- next year

Skill Sharpeners: Geography • EMC 3742 • © Evan-Moor Corp.

New Orleans Then and Now

Look at the photos of New Orleans, Louisiana. What is the same? What is different?

Streetcars on Canal Street, circa 1907

Streetcars on Canal Street, circa 2016

The Uses of Geography

Skill:
Apply content vocabulary in context sentences

Use Vocabulary

Write a word to complete each sentence.

present	past	future

1. The _____ is the time that happened long ago.

2. The _____ is the time that has not happened yet.

3. The _____ is the time that is happening now.

Draw a picture of your:

past	present	future

The Uses of Geography

What Is the Picture?

Skill:
Demonstrate an understanding of geography concepts

Write a word to tell what each picture shows.

present	past	future

_____

_____

_____

The Uses of Geography

Skill:
Apply geography concepts

Places Change

Answer the items.

1. Has your neighborhood changed over time? If so, tell how. If not, tell how you would like it to change in the future.

_____

_____

2. Has your town changed over time? If so, tell how. If not, tell how you would like it to change in the future.

_____

_____

Draw a picture that shows one thing you wrote about.

The Uses of Geography

What's the Difference?

What You Need

- scissors
- glue

What You Do

Cut out the pictures and follow the directions on page 127.

The Uses of Geography

Skill Sharpeners: Geography • EMC 3742 • © Evan-Moor Corp.

Glue each picture of Times Square in New York City under the correct label. Then show someone the pictures and tell them what has changed.

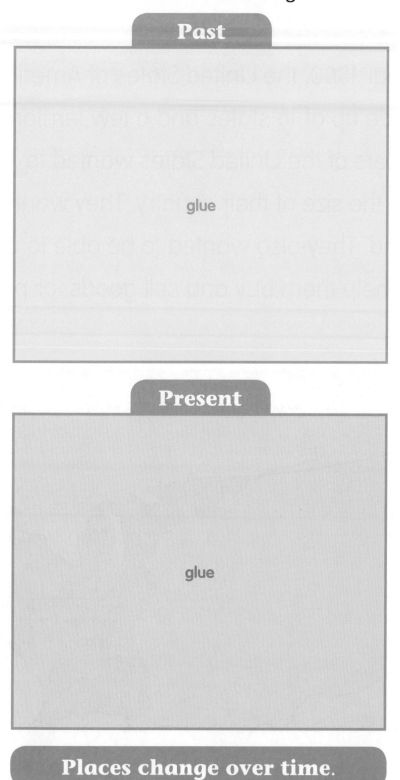

Past

glue

Present

glue

Places change over time.

The Uses of Geography

Skill:
Regions change
over time.

The Size of the United States

In the year 1800, the United States of America was made up of 16 states and a few territories. The leaders of the United States wanted to increase the size of their country. They wanted more land. They also wanted to be able to use rivers to help them buy and sell goods, or products.

This map shows the size of the United States in 1800.

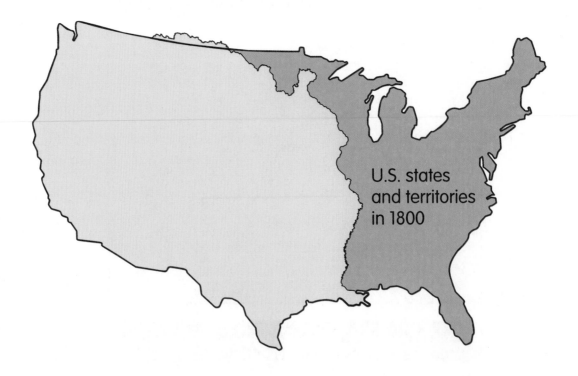

U.S. states and territories in 1800

The Uses of Geography

The Louisiana Purchase

In the year 1803, the United States grew. Thomas Jefferson, the third president of the United States, bought a large area of land to the west. It was called the Louisiana Territory. This purchase doubled the size of the United States. This was not the last change the United States would go through. The United States would continue to grow and change over time.

This map shows the size of the United States in 1803.

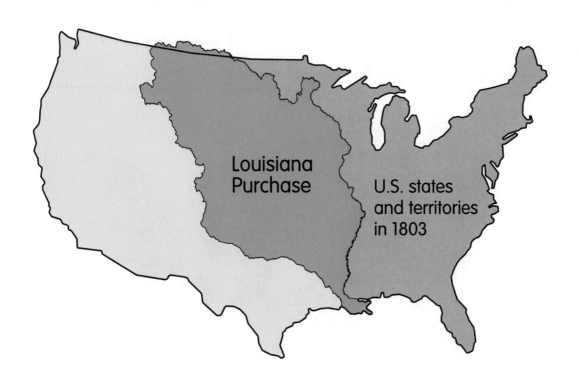

Louisiana Purchase

U.S. states and territories in 1803

The Uses of Geography

Skill:
Apply content vocabulary in context sentences

Use Vocabulary

Write a word or words to complete each sentence.

change	land	Louisiana Purchase

1. The United States wanted more

   _____.

2. The _____ doubled the size of the United States.

3. The United States continued to grow and

   _____ over time.

This is what a map of the United States looks like today. The United States is a country that has changed over time.

The Uses of Geography

Skill Sharpeners: Geography • EMC 3742 • © Evan-Moor Corp.

How the U.S. Has Changed

Skill:
Demonstrate an
understanding
of geography
concepts

Label each map.

1803	1800	today

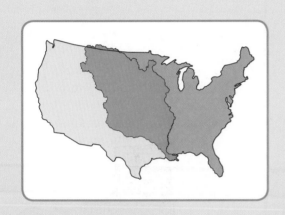

_____

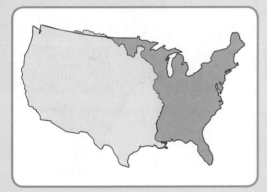

_____

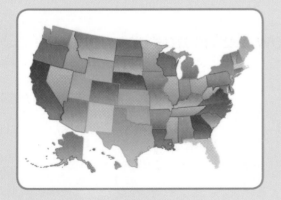

_____

The Uses of Geography

Skill:
Apply geography
concepts

States Can Change Over Time

Look at the maps of the state of Texas. Trace the borders.

Texas is a state in the United States. In 1845, it used to look like this.

Now it looks like this.

Texas

Texas

Circle the words that tell how Texas has changed over time.

shape   name   size

border   rivers

The Uses of Geography

Skill Sharpeners: Geography • EMC 3742 • © Evan-Moor Corp.

An Imaginary Country

What You Need

- scissors
- glue
- colored markers

What You Do

1. Cut out the picture of the imaginary country Zorbis.

2. Glue the map of Zorbis onto page 135 and follow the directions to complete the task.

Zorbis
2018

The Uses of Geography

1. Glue the map of Zorbis below.
2. Read about how the country of Zorbis changed.
3. Draw a picture to show what Zorbis looks like now.

glue

The people who lived in Zorbis wanted it to become a larger country. Some of its borders were round and some were jagged. The people decided to buy the land around Zorbis so its borders would have straight lines. Now the map of Zorbis looks different.

Answer Key

Page 10

Vocabulary

Word Play

Read the clue. Then write the word or words.

1. a direction tells where something is ___
   <u>f o u n d</u>

2. a drawing from above
   <u>m a p</u>

3. a symbol that shows directions
   <u>c o m p a s s   r o s e</u>

4. what **north**, **south**, **east**, and **west** are called
   <u>d i r e c t i o n s</u>

Write the numbered letters to solve the puzzle.

Geography Puzzle

It has symbols that stand for real things.
<u>m a p</u> <u>k e y</u>
 1   2   3   4

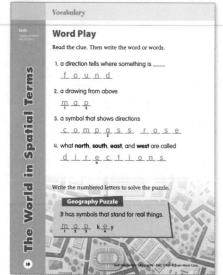

The World in Spatial Terms

Page 11

Visual Literacy

Map Sentences

Mark the sentence that goes with each picture.

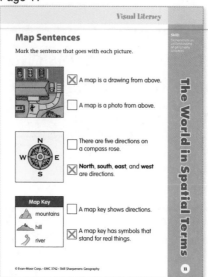

- ☒ A map is a drawing from above.
- ☐ A map is a photo from above.

- ☐ There are five directions on a compass rose.
- ☒ **North**, **south**, **east**, and **west** are directions.

- ☐ A map key shows directions.
- ☒ A map key has symbols that stand for real things.

The World in Spatial Terms

Page 12

What I Learned

I Know About Maps

Write a sentence about each picture.

Answers will vary. Examples:

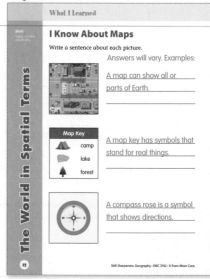

<u>A map can show all or parts of Earth.</u>

Map Key
- camp
- lake
- forest

<u>A map key has symbols that stand for real things.</u>

<u>A compass rose is a symbol that shows directions.</u>

The World in Spatial Terms

Page 18

Vocabulary

About a Globe

Draw a line to match the picture with the correct definition. Then write the word on the line.

| continent | globe | ocean |

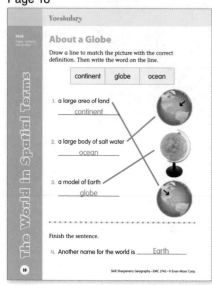

1. a large area of land
   <u>continent</u>

2. a large body of salt water
   <u>ocean</u>

3. a model of Earth
   <u>globe</u>

Finish the sentence.

4. Another name for the world is <u>Earth</u>

The World in Spatial Terms

Page 19

Visual Literacy

What Is the Picture?

Write a word to go with the picture.

| Earth | continent | ocean | globe |

<u>globe</u>   <u>ocean</u>

<u>Earth</u>   <u>continent</u>

The World in Spatial Terms

Page 20

What I Learned

All About the Globe

Label the picture of the globe.

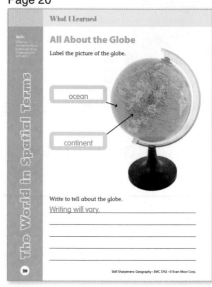

ocean

continent

Write to tell about the globe.

<u>Writing will vary.</u>

The World in Spatial Terms

Page 21

Hands-on Activity

Find a Globe

A globe is round like Earth.

What You Do

1. Find things where you live that look like a globe.
2. Draw them in the box.
3. Write the name of each item below the picture.

Drawings will vary.

The World in Spatial Terms

Page 26

Vocabulary

Use Vocabulary

Write a word to complete each sentence.

| capital | border | city | river |

1. A <u>river</u> is a large stream of water that flows across land.
2. Columbus is the <u>capital</u> of Ohio.
3. A <u>border</u> shows where a place begins and ends.
4. A <u>city</u> is a large or important town.

Trace the grid.

Draw a △ in **A2**.

Draw a ☆ in **D1**.

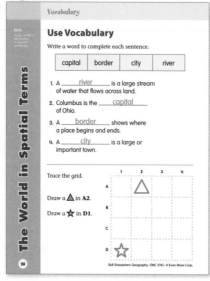

The World in Spatial Terms

Page 27

Visual Literacy

Using a Map Grid

Use the map grid to answer the questions.

1. What animals are in **C4**? <u>alligators</u>
2. What animals are in **B2**? <u>hippos</u>
3. Where is the entrance? <u>D2</u>
4. Where can you buy ice cream? <u>B4</u>
5. Trace the square around the tigers.

The World in Spatial Terms

Page 28

Page 31

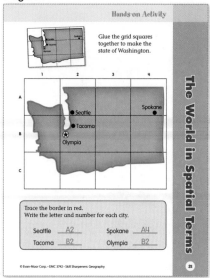

Page 34

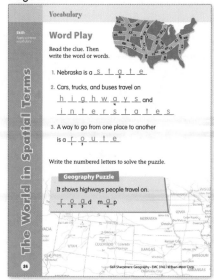

Page 35

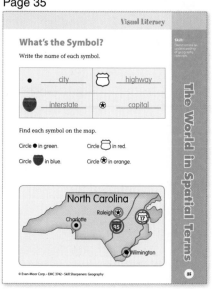

Page 36

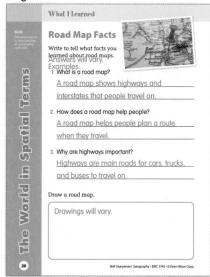

Page 39

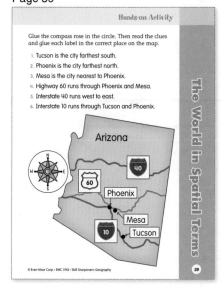

Page 42

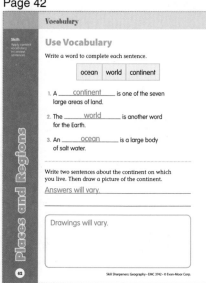

Page 43

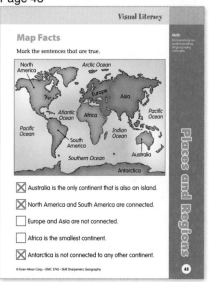

Page 44

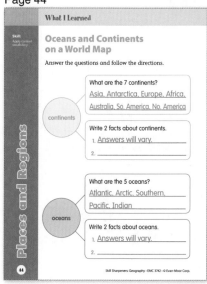

Page 47

Glue each continent in the correct place.

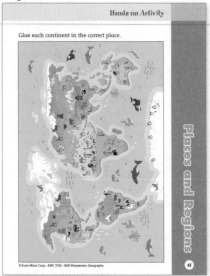

47

Places and Regions

Page 50

Skill: Apply content vocabulary

About a Land and Water Map

Write a word to match each picture and definition.

landform	river	sound	volcano

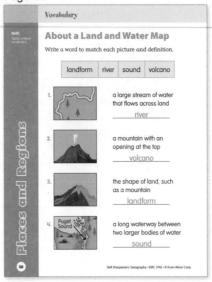

1. a large stream of water that flows across land
   <u>river</u>

2. a mountain with an opening at the top
   <u>volcano</u>

3. the shape of land, such as a mountain
   <u>landform</u>

4. a long waterway between two larger bodies of water
   <u>sound</u>

50

Places and Regions

Page 51

Using a Land and Water Map

Use the map to answer the questions.

Skill: Apply geography concepts

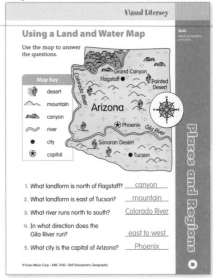

1. What landform is north of Flagstaff? <u>canyon</u>
2. What landform is east of Tucson? <u>mountain</u>
3. What river runs north to south? <u>Colorado River</u>
4. In what direction does the Gila River run? <u>east to west</u>
5. What city is the capital of Arizona? <u>Phoenix</u>

51

Places and Regions

Page 52

Skill: Demonstrate an understanding of geography concepts

All About a Land and Water Map

Label the picture of the map.

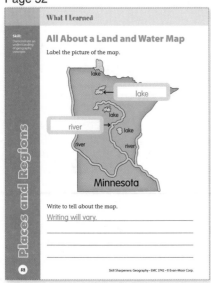

Write to tell about the map.

<u>Writing will vary.</u>

Places and Regions

52

Page 55

Sort the pictures into landforms and bodies of water. Then glue the pictures in the boxes and complete the sentences.

You might see these <u>landforms</u> on a map.

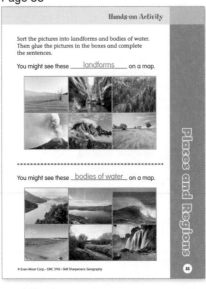

You might see these <u>bodies of water</u> on a map.

55

Places and Regions

Page 58

Skill: Apply content vocabulary

Word Play

Read the clue. Then write the word.

1. a large or important town
   <u>c i t y</u>
   1   5

2. a community near a city
   <u>s u b u r b</u>
   3

3. a very tall building
   <u>s k y s c r a p e r</u>
   5

4. a city's main business area
   <u>d o w n t o w n</u>
   2   4   6

Write the numbered letters to solve the puzzle.

Geography Puzzle

It is a group of people who live together in the same area.

<u>c o mm u n i t y</u>
1   2   3   4   5   6   7

58

Places and Regions

Page 59

What Is the Picture?

Write a word to go with the picture.

Skill: Apply content vocabulary

downtown	skyscrapers	city	suburb

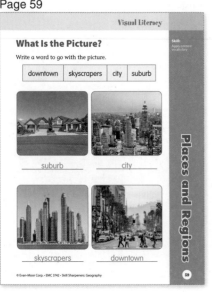

<u>suburb</u>   <u>city</u>

<u>skyscrapers</u>   <u>downtown</u>

59

Places and Regions

Page 60

Skill: Demonstrate an understanding of geography concepts

Places People Live and Work

Write a sentence about each picture.

Answers will vary. Examples:

<u>A city is a large or important town.</u>

<u>A skyscraper is a tall building in a city.</u>

<u>A suburb is a community near a city.</u>

60

Places and Regions

Page 63

This is a suburb.

This is a city.

63

Places and Regions

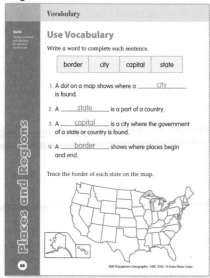

Vocabulary

Use Vocabulary

Write a word to complete each sentence.

| border | city | capital | state |

1. A dot on a map shows where a _____ city _____ is found.

2. A _____ state _____ is a part of a country.

3. A _____ capital _____ is a city where the government of a state or country is found.

4. A _____ border _____ shows where places begin and end.

Trace the border of each state on the map.

Places and Regions

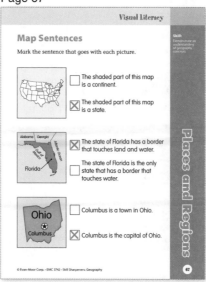

Visual Literacy

Map Sentences

Mark the sentence that goes with each picture.

☐ The shaded part of this map is a continent.
☒ The shaded part of this map is a state.

☒ The state of Florida has a border that touches land and water.
☐ The state of Florida is the only state that has a border that touches water.

☐ Columbus is a town in Ohio.
☒ Columbus is the capital of Ohio.

Places and Regions

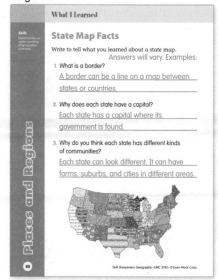

What I Learned

State Map Facts

Write to tell what you learned about a state map.
Answers will vary. Examples:

1. What is a border?
   A border can be a line on a map between states or countries.

2. Why does each state have a capital?
   Each state has a capital where its government is found.

3. Why do you think each state has different kinds of communities?
   Each state can look different. It can have farms, suburbs, and cities in different areas.

Places and Regions

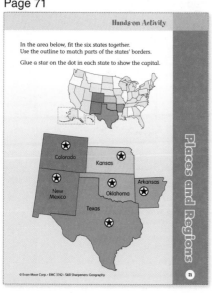

Hands-on Activity

In the area below, fit the six states together. Use the outline to match parts of the states' borders.

Glue a star on the dot in each state to show the capital.

Colorado Kansas New Mexico Oklahoma Arkansas Texas

Places and Regions

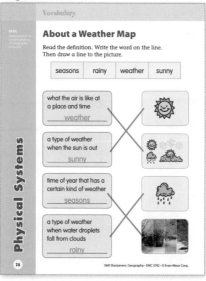

Vocabulary

About a Weather Map

Read the definition. Write the word on the line. Then draw a line to the picture.

| seasons | rainy | weather | sunny |

what the air is like at a place and time
weather

a type of weather when the sun is out
sunny

time of year that has a certain kind of weather
seasons

a type of weather when water droplets fall from clouds
rainy

Physical Systems

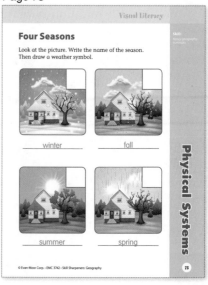

Visual Literacy

Four Seasons

Look at the picture. Write the name of the season. Then draw a weather symbol.

winter   fall

summer   spring

Physical Systems

What I Learned

Weather and Seasons

Answer the questions and follow the directions.

weather

What are the different kinds of weather?
sunny   rainy
partly cloudy   snowy

Write something you know about weather.
Answers will vary.

seasons

What are the 4 seasons?
summer   winter
fall   spring

Write something you know about seasons.
Answers will vary.

Physical Systems

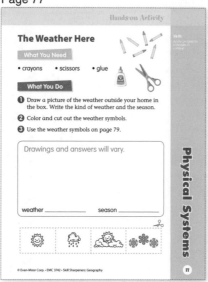

Hands-on Activity

The Weather Here

What You Need
• crayons   • scissors   • glue

What You Do
1. Draw a picture of the weather outside your home in the box. Write the kind of weather and the season.
2. Color and cut out the weather symbols.
3. Use the weather symbols on page 79.

Drawings and answers will vary.

weather _____   season _____

Physical Systems

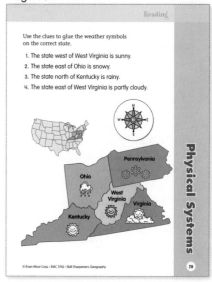

Reading

Use the clues to glue the weather symbols on the correct state.

1. The state west of West Virginia is sunny.
2. The state east of Ohio is snowy.
3. The state north of Kentucky is rainy.
4. The state east of West Virginia is partly cloudy.

Pennsylvania Ohio West Virginia Virginia Kentucky

Physical Systems

Page 82

Word Play

Read the clue. Then write the word or words.

1. they bring water to tide pools
   w a v e s

2. when plants and animals are dry
   l o w   t i d e

3. kelp gets nutrients through this
   b l a d e

4. its trees are under the water
   k e l p   f o r e s t

Write the numbered letters to solve the puzzle.

Geography Puzzle

It is where the shore and the ocean meet.
t i d e   p o o l s

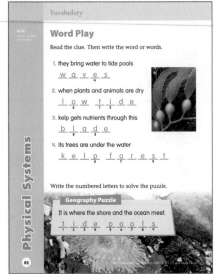

Physical Systems

Page 83

Habitat Sentences

Mark the sentence that goes with each picture.

- ☒ Tide pools are found where the shore and the ocean meet.
- ☐ Tide pools are found in the middle of the ocean.

- ☒ Many animals live in kelp forests.
- ☐ Only sea stars live in kelp forests.

- ☐ Sea otters live in tide pools.
- ☒ Sea otters live in kelp forests.

Physical Systems

Page 84

It Looks Like This...

Read the sentence. Then draw a picture to match it.

Drawings will vary.

A tide pool is where the shore and the ocean meet.

Kelp is a plant in the ocean.

The ocean is a habitat to many plants and animals.

Physical Systems

Page 87

This is an ocean habitat.

Collages will vary.

Physical Systems

Page 90

Word Play

Read the clue. Then write the word.

1. the total number of people who live in a place
   p o p u l a t i o n

2. a large town   c i t y

3. a group of people who help make laws
   g o v e r n m e n t

4. a city where the government of a state or country is found   c a p i t a l

5. the capital of Kansas
   T o p e k a

Write the numbered letters to solve the puzzle.

Geography Puzzle

It is a reason population changes over time.
p e o p l e   m o v e

Human Systems

Page 91

Using a Population Map

Use the map to answer the items.

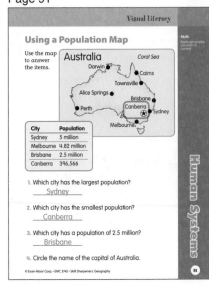

Australia

City	Population
Sydney	5 million
Melbourne	4.82 million
Brisbane	2.5 million
Canberra	396,566

1. Which city has the largest population?
   Sydney

2. Which city has the smallest population?
   Canberra

3. Which city has a population of 2.5 million?
   Brisbane

4. Circle the name of the capital of Australia.

Human Systems

Page 92

All About a Population Map

Look at the map symbols.
Write **capital** and **city** to label the map of Pennsylvania.
Then read the population information.

Pennsylvania

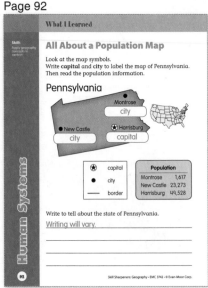

Montrose — city
New Castle — city
Harrisburg — capital

★ capital
● city
— border

Population	
Montrose	1,617
New Castle	23,273
Harrisburg	49,528

Write to tell about the state of Pennsylvania.
Writing will vary.

Human Systems

Page 95

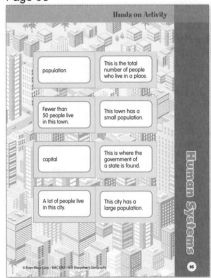

population — This is the total number of people who live in a place.

Fewer than 50 people live in this town. — This town has a small population.

capital — This is where the government of a state is found.

A lot of people live in this city. — This city has a large population.

Human Systems

Page 98

Products

Write a word or words to complete each sentence.

| crops | livestock | cattle | product map |

1. A product map shows where things such as crops and livestock are found.

2. Crops are plants farmers grow for food and to sell for money.

3. Cattle are cows, bulls, and steers that are raised on a farm or ranch.

4. Livestock are animals raised on a farm or ranch. Livestock are sold for money.

Answer the item.

Is this a product map?
● yes   ○ no

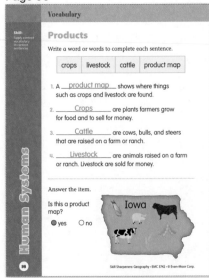

Iowa

Human Systems

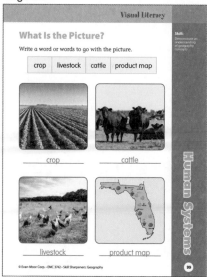

Visual Literacy

What Is the Picture?

Write a word or words to go with the picture.

| crop | livestock | cattle | product map |

crop · cattle

livestock · product map

Human Systems

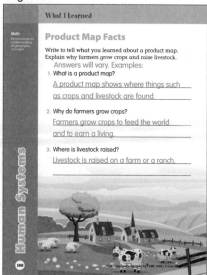

What I Learned

Product Map Facts

Write to tell what you learned about a product map. Explain why farmers grow crops and raise livestock.

Answers will vary. Examples:

1. What is a product map?
   A product map shows where things such as crops and livestock are found.

2. Why do farmers grow crops?
   Farmers grow crops to feed the world and to earn a living.

3. Where is livestock raised?
   Livestock is raised on a farm or a ranch.

Human Systems

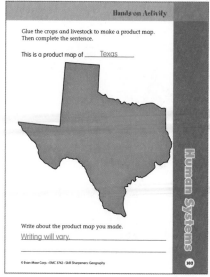

Hands-on Activity

Glue the crops and livestock to make a product map. Then complete the sentence.

This is a product map of ___Texas___

Write about the product map you made.
Writing will vary.

Human Systems

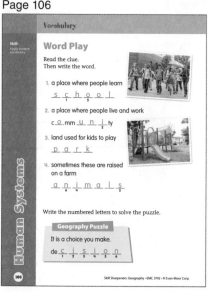

Vocabulary

Word Play

Read the clue. Then write the word.

1. a place where people learn
   s c h o o l

2. a place where people live and work
   c o mm u n i ty

3. land used for kids to play
   p a r k

4. sometimes these are raised on a farm
   a n i m a l s

Write the numbered letters to solve the puzzle.

Geography Puzzle

It is a choice you make.
de c i s i o n

Human Systems

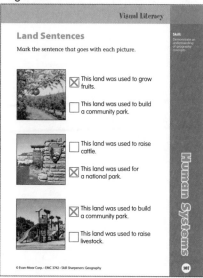

Visual Literacy

Land Sentences

Mark the sentence that goes with each picture.

☒ This land was used to grow fruits.
☐ This land was used to build a community park.

☐ This land was used to raise cattle.
☒ This land was used for a national park.

☒ This land was used to build a community park.
☐ This land was used to raise livestock.

Human Systems

What I Learned

All About How Land Is Used

Draw a picture of one way your community uses land.

Drawings will vary.

Write to tell about your picture.
Writing will vary.

Human Systems

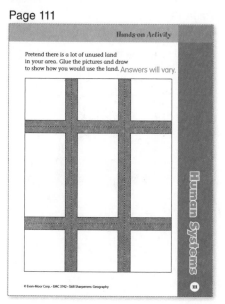

Hands-on Activity

Pretend there is a lot of unused land in your area. Glue the pictures and draw to show how you would use the land. Answers will vary.

Human Systems

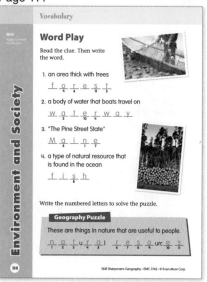

Vocabulary

Word Play

Read the clue. Then write the word.

1. an area thick with trees
   f o r e s t

2. a body of water that boats travel on
   w a t e r w a y

3. "The Pine Street State"
   M a i n e

4. a type of natural resource that is found in the ocean
   f i s h

Write the numbered letters to solve the puzzle.

Geography Puzzle

These are things in nature that are useful to people.
n a t u r a l r e s o urc e s

Environment and Society

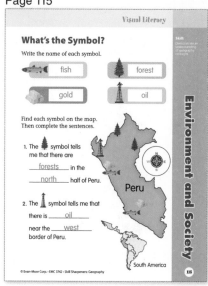

Visual Literacy

What's the Symbol?

Write the name of each symbol.

fish · forest
gold · oil

Find each symbol on the map. Then complete the sentences.

1. The 🌲 symbol tells me that there are
   forests in the
   north half of Peru.

2. The symbol tells me that
   there is oil
   near the west
   border of Peru.

Peru

South America

Environment and Society

Page 116

Getting Natural Resources

Write a sentence about each picture.

Answers will vary. Examples:
These men are catching many
fish in a net. They will eat
them or sell them.

These logs were cut down
from a forest. They will be
used to make things.

Read. Then answer the question.

This is an oil drilling rig. It is drilling for oil. Oil rigs can be seen all over the world. Have you ever seen an oil drilling rig? Tell where.

Answers will vary.

Environment and Society

Page 119

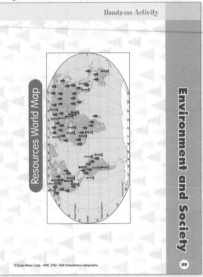

Resources World Map

Environment and Society

Page 122

Use Vocabulary

Write a word to complete each sentence.

present	past	future

1. The ___past___ is the time that happened long ago.

2. The ___future___ is the time that has not happened yet.

3. The ___present___ is the time that is happening now.

Draw a picture of your:

past	present	future
Drawings will vary.		

The Uses of Geography

Page 123

What Is the Picture?

Write a word to tell what each picture shows.

present	past	future

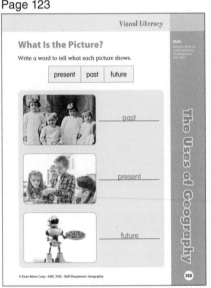

past

present

future

The Uses of Geography

Page 124

Places Change

Answer the items.

1. Has your neighborhood changed over time? If so, tell how. If not, tell how you would like it to change in the future.

   Answers will vary.

2. Has your town changed over time? If so, tell how. If not, tell how you would like it to change in the future.

   Answers will vary.

Draw a picture that shows one thing you wrote about.

Drawings will vary.

The Uses of Geography

Page 127

Glue each picture of Times Square in New York City under the correct label. Then show someone the pictures and tell them what has changed.

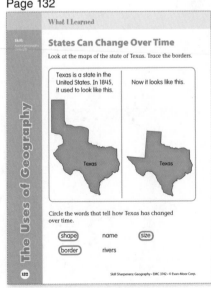

Past

Present

Places change over time.

The Uses of Geography

Page 130

Use Vocabulary

Write a word or words to complete each sentence.

change	land	Louisiana Purchase

1. The United States wanted more ___land___

2. The ___Louisiana Purchase___ doubled the size of the United States.

3. The United States continued to grow and ___change___ over time.

This is what a map of the United States looks like today. The United States is a country that has changed over time.

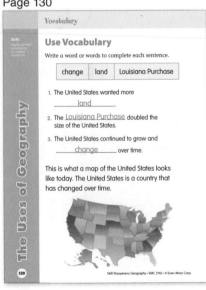

The Uses of Geography

Page 131

How the U.S. Has Changed

Label each map.

1803	1800	today

1803

1800

today

The Uses of Geography

Page 132

States Can Change Over Time

Look at the maps of the state of Texas. Trace the borders.

Texas is a state in the United States. In 1845, it used to look like this.

Now it looks like this.

Texas

Texas

Circle the words that tell how Texas has changed over time.

shape   name   size

border   rivers

The Uses of Geography
